The Audacity of Faith

The Audacity of Faith

✦

The Relevance of Faith to Success

Emma S. Etuk, PhD

iUniverse, Inc.

New York   Bloomington

iUniverse books may be ordered through booksellers or by contacting:

iUniverse
1663 Liberty Drive
Bloomington, IN 47403
www.iuniverse.com
1-800-Authors (1-800-288-4677)

Because of the dynamic nature of the Internet, any Web addresses or links
contained in this book may have changed since publication and may no longer be
valid. The views expressed in this work are solely those of the author and do not
necessarily reflect the views of the publisher, and the publisher hereby disclaims
any responsibility for them.

ISBN: 978-1-4401-8608-0 (sc)
ISBN: 978-1-4401-8607-3 (ebook)

Printed in the United States of America

iUniverse rev. date:11/18/2009

Advance Praise for The Audacity of Faith

During my evangelistic and pastoral ministries in Ghana, West Africa, the United States, as well as in other parts of the world for fifty years, I have noticed a general trend of doubt, discouragement, perplexity, fear, and anger that have crept into many lives. There is also intrusive fear that is gripping men and women of the present world because of terror, disease, disaster, pain, and suffering. In the[se] circumstances, therefore, many people are unable to believe for the impossible.

Dr. Etuk has given a vivid description of the audacity of faith and what it can do in the lives of those who are able to exercise it. Adding a copy of the book to your library will be a great blessing to you and your family.

—Rev. Dr. Stephen K. Gyermeh, Senior Pastor, Founder, General Overseer, Church of the Living God Full Gospel Ministries

If you're going to read one book this year on faith, read the Bible. If you're going to read more than one book, then I would strongly recommend The Audacity of Faith. Dr. Etuk has written an accessible, yet profound treatise about Christian faith and why faith matters in the midst of global economic meltdown. Dr. Etuk has also written with a palpable sense of urgency that our faith requires of us in time of fear and uncertainty. This book will be an encouragement to all who seek answers in time of despair.

—Stephen Onu,
Associate Professor, Global Management, Western
International University

A book, like an award, is as good as its source. Dr. Emma Etuk has demonstrated with several well-regarded books he has authored that he writes from the heart to inspire, guide, and change lives. Visibly swimming in the currents of the Obama phenomenon, The Audacity of Faith is a pathfinder atlas of Christian living, an invaluable companion on your way to the mountaintop.

—Rev, C. Paschal Eze,
Author, Certified Training Consultant, Founder
AfricaResults.com

Dr. Emma Etuk has kept his sense of commitment to recording the African experience in America and beyond. In this book, his eleventh publication, he captures the feelings and dreams of many persons of African origin who see in the 2008 electoral victory of President Obama the beginning of a new day in America and the world.

To Etuk, the Obama victory and the trend of developments now taking place, have reassured him about the meaning of audacity. Looking into this term and the concept it stands for, Dr. Etuk is raising the flag of optimism and hope, and he thinks many human beings, especially Africans bitten by the bug of Obamaphilia, are going to succeed.

He is historically conscious and he uses the writings of colleagues in that and other disciplines to make his point. Many will find this book useful and the other works of the author hopefully will be read with equal enthusiasm.

—Sulayman S. Nyang, PhD
Howard University, Washington DC

As a physician, I have witnessed to the immeasurable power of faith and the role it plays in the healing process. Patients with a firm spiritual foundation are much more optimistic and less fearful about their condition. This faith gives them the fortitude to persevere and clearly improves outcomes.

In Dr. Etuk's eloquent, concisely written book, we are given tremendous insight into the importance of courage and faith as we face the realities of today's world. Through the eyes of our past and present leaders, Dr. Etuk has provided us with inspiration and allowed us to glimpse a vision of ourselves as making a positive difference wherever we serve.

—Alyson L. Hall, MD,
President, The Glaucoma Center, P.C.

To Professor Sulayman Nyang, my mentor and friend,
For his persistent support and encouragement in this work of
authorship.

Contents

Acknowledgments

My thanks are due to a host of people who have aided me in this piece of work. Among them are the blurb writers: Dr. Sulayman Nyang, Reverend Dr. Stephen K. Gyermeh, Stephen Onu, Reverend C. Paschal, and Alyson L. Hall, MD.

Without the following financial supporters, especially when my computer failed me, I would not have been able to complete this work: Daniel Gyermeh, Dr. Sulayman Nyang, Brother Isaac Larbi, and others who choose to remain anonymous.

I am indeed happy to be associated with Frank of the *BusinessDay* newspaper in Lagos, Nigeria, whose generosity and business premises offered to me the opportunity to publicly present the spoken version of this work. It was the happy reception of that address by him and his staff that urged me to think of turning the speech into a book.

Finally, I am indebted to my family, both in Lagos and in America, for their constant support. I could not have become an incorrigible and persistent writer without their help. May God richly bless you all.

CHAPTER ONE

✦

Introduction

The word *audacity* has been recently popularized by the U.S. president, Barack Obama, in his 2006 best-selling book, *The Audacity of Hope*. The genesis of Obama's book was the keynote address he presented at the 2004 Democratic National Convention (DNC) in Boston, Massachusetts. The address brought Obama national attention.[1]

We now have many writers on the topic of audacity. The Nigerian media alone provided not less than six such writers. "The Audacity of Dreams,"[2] an article that appeared in a Nigerian newspaper, is the story of Cosmas Maduka, a Nigerian business guru who wanted to own a company like Leventis Group. Maduka wrote: "If you do not believe that there is a way if you have the will, ask Americans to tell you about a man called Obama."[3] On January 20 2009, Obama was inaugurated as the 44th president of the United States, the first black to be elected president in the United States.

A sermon by Felix Meduoye titled "The Audacity of Faith"[4] points to the faith exemplified by three ancient Hebrew young men in captivity. The young men were known as Shadrach, Meschach, and Abednego. Their story is found in the Bible (Daniel 3:17–18).

Meduoye also examined the case of another slave called Daniel, who rose from slavery to power. He also spoke about a woman with an issue of blood who was healed by the audacity of her faith (Matthew 9:20). According to Meduoye, the historical King David rose from grass to greatness by the audacity of his faith.

In yet another article titled "Audacity of Corruption: U.S. vs. Nigeria,"[5] a journalist named Minabere Ibelema made the observation that, despite the differences in size and longevity between the United States and Nigeria, the "audacity of corruption" persists in both countries.

In the United States, three persons—a governor, a mayor, and a senator—were indicted on charges of alleged corruption. In Nigeria, however, corruption is typically characterized by *kleptocracy*, which is the stealing of billions in government money, and it is "pervasive." Rarely do the culprits in Nigeria get convicted or imprisoned. So, Ibelema concluded that the campaign against corruption in Nigeria could only ameliorate the issue, not obliterate it.

In one article entitled "Audacity of Hope: Can It Happen Here?"[6] four Nigerian journalists offered the opinions from a national survey that they had conducted. They had interviewed some "notable Nigerians" on the subject of power change. The interviewees included state governors and lawmakers.

The survey revealed, "something was fundamentally wrong with most African countries."[7] That something is the inability of their governments to hand over power to the next government, peacefully. Cynicism is rampant because of this lack of peaceful change. To use the words of ex-president Olusegun Obasanjo, in Africa, politics is a "do-or-die" business.

In her article titled, "Nigeria: 'The Audacity of Hope,'"[8] Karen C. Aboiralor provides an upbeat and positive assessment of the Nigerian situation; she admits that she is an optimist. After painting a gloomy picture of Nigeria, Aboiralor writes that Obama won his election in the United States because of his qualities of hard work, diligence, dedication to duty, careful planning, and optimism. In her words: "Obama worked for his success." This is the lesson that Abioralor wants her fellow Nigerians to learn from the United States. But she also believes that the Nigerian condition may get worse before things begin to get better.

Aboiralor concluded her article by stating that "it is clearly in the interest of the ruling elite to govern better or they themselves will be consumed by the rising anger of the impoverished populace."[9]

On December 4, 2008, exactly one month after the election of Obama, this writer spoke at the offices of *Business Day Nigeria*, a newspaper in Lagos. The subject of the speech was "The Audacity of Faith, or the Relevance of Faith to Success." He was invited by Frank Aigbogun, the newspaper's CEO, to offer a motivational address to the workers of the company.

The address was later published.[10] Aboiralor's article and the address became the genesis for this book which you are now reading. We are all greatly indebted to President Barack Obama. The next chapter examines the general meaning of the term *audacity*. Read on.

CHAPTER TWO

✦

What Is Audacity?

In order that we might properly understand the subject under discussion, we ought to ask ourselves the question, "What is audacity?" There are at least six other words or terms that can explain what audacity is. The first of these is *courage*.

The dictionary says that audacity is "the quality of having enough courage to take risks or say impolite things."[1] At the same time, this definition adds that audacity means "to be brave and shocking."[2] Thus, *bravery* is our second word.

The third is *temerity*. It is an "unreasonable confidence that is likely to offend someone."[3] It is important to point out here that this apparent "unreasonable(ness)" depends upon one's own perspective. I do not believe that a person who is audacious thinks that he or she is unreasonable in his or her actions.

The fourth word that offers something close to the meaning of audacity is *effrontery*, defined as "behavior that you think someone should be ashamed of, although they do not seem to be."[4] Given the particular kind of behavior, an audacious person need not be ashamed for being audacious. Otherwise, how then can he or she be audacious?

The fifth term that helps us to understand what audacity means is *guts*. It is defined as "the courage and determination you need to do something difficult or unpleasant."[5] Audacious people are people with the guts for action. They do not sit idly and just wish that something good might happen to them. No, sir; they take action however perilous and difficult the task may be. They are the go-getters.

In the Bible, Esther represented this kind of person when, in her decision to meet with the king at a time of national crisis, she resolved: "If I perish, I perish" (Esther 4:16). Now, in retrospect, did her decision and action appear "unreasonable?" You bet. Apparently, she was making an unprecedented, unnecessary, and dangerous decision. Although it was a difficult and unpleasant decision, she was a woman with guts. She possessed the audacity to meet the king, in violation of a royal decree!

The sixth word is unusual *boldness* that may seem offensive to the beholder. Esther, again, displayed such a quality. The celebrated Nigerian pastor and General Overseer of the Deeper Life Christian Ministries, Reverend W. F. Kumuyi, told a story of a person who had unusual boldness.

"One day," wrote Kumuyi, "a soldier assisted Napoleon when his horse became unmanageable. The great general said. 'Thank you, *Captain!*' The soldier immediately took him at his word, and said: 'Of what regiment, sir?' Napoleon, pleased at his sharp perception and ready trust, replied: 'Of my guard.'"[6]

Napoleon rode away, but the soldier promptly went to the staff officers and announced to them that he was the Captain of Napoleon's Guards. It took an unusual boldness to do so knowing that his fellow soldiers would not believe him.

What, then, is audacity? It is the possession and exercise of the virtues of courage, bravery, temerity, effrontery, guts, and unusual boldness *to do* the unbelievable. It is faith triumphing over fear and doubts. Audacity will produce a tenacity (the knack or daring attitude), which is often sustained by persistence and perseverance.

Audacity is the willingness and ability to take risks with a confidence that may likely offend someone else. It is the quality exemplified by the young shepherd boy, David, when he was about to take on Goliath, the Philistine. Surely, David offended his older brothers who were regular soldiers in King Saul's military.

But, David had the audacity to seek permission from King Saul to take on Goliath. *And he did.* That kind of audacity generally produces men and women of significance and greatness. It produces men and women of success.

In our time, it has produced Barack Hussein Obama, who has shown the world that he could do what appeared to be impossible: run for the presidency of the United States as an African American and win. Barack Obama is a man with an audacious spirit.

He is now the 44th president of the United States, America's first black president ever! All peoples of his race are very proud of him. With one stroke, Obama has wiped out the curse of the language of racial inferiority from future textbooks.

CHAPTER THREE

✦

What Is Faith?

Faith is the opposite of fear.

—*Emma S. Etuk*

There may be many definitions of the word faith, but the best
that I have found is in the Christian Bible. There, in the book of
Hebrews, the eleventh chapter, verse 1, it says:

Now, faith *is* the *substance* of things hoped for, the *evidence* of
things not yet seen. (Italics added)

Now, you have to ponder on and think carefully what this
text really says and means. This text does not say that faith is
an abstraction, a will-o'-the-wisp; it says that faith is a *substance*.
Moreover, the text does not say that faith is a figment of one's own
imagination, a product of sheer human reasoning; it says that faith
is the *evidence* of the things not yet seen.

At verse six of the text, the Bible states that,

Without faith, it is impossible to please God.

In other words, faith—authentic, biblical faith—is rooted in
the supernatural. In another book of the Bible, believed to have
been authored by St. Paul, it is recorded that "whatsoever is not
of faith is sin" (Rom.14:36). This is a very strong and powerful
statement worthy of serious consideration.

In Romans 1:17 and Habakkuk 2:4, the Bible says that "the
just shall live by faith." You may recall that the discovery of the
text in Romans by the German priest, Martin Luther, led to

the Protestant Reformation, which swept across Europe in the sixteenth century.

Faith is a dynamic, creative force in the universe.[2] The Scriptures say that "through faith we understand that the worlds were framed by the word of God" (Heb. 11:3). We cannot scientifically prove all the creative works of God; we have to accept them by faith. Thus, faith is a catalyst that leads to *action* and produces a product, a *substance* of the things hoped for.

It is important to always keep in mind this other fact, namely, that without *action*, faith is dead (James 2:26). Yet without faith, it is impossible to accomplish much. Hence, one cannot succeed without faith. Happily, the Bible also says that God has given to each of us a measure of faith. Therefore no one can claim that he or she is completely without faith (Rom. 12:3).

Jesus often taught that faith is crucial in our daily life. He made the incredible statement that if one had faith as little as that of a mustard seed, one can move mountains! One can do the impossible through and by faith (Matt. 17:20).

People of faith do nearly impossible things. I said "nearly impossible" because, actually, there are no impossibilities. "All things are possible to him who believes," Jesus said (Mk. 9:23).

THE FAITH PROCESS

It should by now be obvious that faith involves a process.[3] There are categories and varieties of faith. Let's look at a few:

- Saving faith (Rom. 10:9,10)
- Little (small) faith (Mt. 8:26; 17:20)
- Great faith (Mt. 8:10)
- Temporary faith (Lk. 8:13)
- Intellectual faith (James 2:19)
- Dead faith (James 2:17, 20)
- Faith of the Son of God (Gal. 2:20)
- Strong faith (Rom. 4:20)

A person has the ability to develop his or her faith, implying that there can be a growth in faith. This may explain why some people achieve and succeed much more than others. It is recommended here that we must appraise the level of our faith from time to time.

The Faith Practice

Faith, like prayer, does not need proof; it needs practice.[4] By this, I mean that you exercise your faith by getting it into action. Faith has to be *ignited* always if you want to see its power and concrete results.[5]

The Bible speaks of many faith practitioners who attested to the workability of faith. For example, the Bible says that the prophet Elijah was a man like us, but he was also a man of tremendous faith who, through earnest prayers, shut up the heavens so that it did not rain for three years. Later on, he prayed again, and it rained (James 5:17–18).

At an encounter with the agnostics, skeptics, and, perhaps, the atheists of his day, Elijah called down fire from heaven to lick up a watery evening sacrifice, to the amazement and wonder of the onlookers (I Kings 17–18: 45). It is no wonder that his God had to transport him back to heaven in a chariot of fire. *He did not see death.*

Elijah's successor in office, Elisha, did even more miracles than him by the audacity of faith. He raised dead people back to life. He even caused an iron axe to float or swim. He healed poisonous water and made it drinkable once more. After Elisha died, some years later a dead man who was dropped accidentally on his grave's bones rose back to life! (II Kings 13:21)

In the book of Hebrews, chapter 11, we have a catalog of great faith-workers who accomplished incredible things. They include the patriarch and father of faith, Abraham; Abel; Enoch (another man who never tasted death); Noah; Isaac and his son,

Jacob; Sarah, Abraham's wife; Joseph; and Moses, the great Jewish lawgiver.

Among others were those Hebrews who actually crossed the Red Sea; Joshua and Caleb, who captured Jericho; Rahab, the harlot; Gideon; Barak; Samson; Jephthah; David; Samuel; and many, many prophets. The great exploits of these men and women are recorded in Hebrews 11:33–38.

Only the theologically insane would dare to say that all these men and women simply represented mythological Jewish legends. But, even if they were just legends, what of the following faith workers of our own time, such as

- Oral Roberts
- T. L. Osborne
- Morris Cerullo
- Kathryn Kuhlman
- Benny Hinn
- Uma Ukpai
- Rev. O. Ezekiel
- Pastor W. F. Kumuyi

and a host of many others? What of the evangelist Reinhard Bonnke? Are they all "fake" faith workers? Are you really sure? What makes you so absolutely sure?

If, as the Bible claims, "Jesus Christ [is] the same yesterday, today and forever" (Heb. 13: 8), then faith in His name can produce the same results as it did in Bible times. This is simply logical. Faith in God can lead to great achievements in all the areas of life. God is not limited to any one circumstance or to any one historical epoch.

As the book of the Acts of the Apostles shows, anyone with faith in God can move mountains. This is the hard fact about God. He is unchangeable. Jesus said that with God, nothing is impossible. We must always bear in mind that *without faith, it is impossible to please God.* Faith comes by hearing the Word of God and *trusting* that whatever He says is always true.

It is by the *ignition* of faith that *action* occurs. You and I will never attempt nor achieve great things without faith. Faith is the dynamite for successful living. We have to embrace it as we would intimately embrace our spouse.

CHAPTER FOUR

✦

The Secret of Faith

It may not be quite obvious to many faith-seekers that the secret of faith is simply *belief.* In the text that we have been studying (Heb. 11:6), there is hidden the secret of faith. The passage reads as follows:

Whoever comes to God must believe that He is (exists).

Get it? Anyone who wants to know anything about God must first of all believe that God exists! Not only does He exist, He has revealed Himself; He has spoken. We do not worship a dumb and deaf God. Then there is an addition: God is the rewarder of those who diligently seek Him.

By the above rule, atheists—that is, those who profess that God does not exist—stand no chance at all unless they change their mindset. I often wonder how an atheist perfectly knows and is sure that there is no God; the atheist has to be omniscient in order to be absolutely sure of this.

Furthermore, the atheist has to be omnipresent. For, at the corner of the universe where the atheist does not exist, God may be hiding! It is no wonder, then, that the Bible says, "The fool has said in his heart, there is no God" (Psalm 14:1; 10:4, 6). The Bible calls the atheists "empty-headed" fools.

I have to stress the point that authentic, dynamic, faith must be grounded in the supernatural, in the divine, in the God who created all things and sustains the earth by His power. One must follow the example of Anselm of Canterbury, an early church father, who penned the dictum *credo ut intelligam*, meaning, "I believe in order that I may understand."

Thus, we are back to the word, *belief.* But what is belief? Jesus often urged His hearers to believe. The word belief is a noun, a New Testament translation of the word *trust* in the Old Testament. In the Amplified version of the Bible, believe is rendered as *cleaving* to, *trusting* in, *relying* on, and *clinging* to (John 3: 15–16). Belief also includes adherence to the Word of God (Rom. 10:9).

You must believe or trust, rely, have the confidence, maintain a level of personal assurance, that whatever you are doing right now has the potential to lift you up to a new level of greatness. Otherwise, you are simply wasting your precious time. Cease from doing that which is routine and a waste of time.

Your faith ought to take you to somewhere—to the top! As American author and foremost motivational speaker Zig Ziglar would say, "See you at the top."[1] There is always more room at the top.

The Four Faces of Faith

According to Stephen Mansfield, the author of <u>The Faith of Barack Obama</u> (2008), there are four faces of faith that are discernible at the American political platform:

1. The John McCain, Episcopalian kind of faith, rooted in the faith of his fathers, a faith in the love of God and country, duty and patriotism. In this kind of faith, one sees, as McCain did, "religion as the power behind character, as the fuel of right behavior."[2]
2. The George H. W. Bush kind of faith, also an Episcopalian, who did not easily speak of his personal religion.[3]
3. The Hillary Clinton kind of faith, representing Wesleyan Methodism, the "generation of spiritual seekers,"[4] of the post–World War II era, who combined the gospel with a social conscience.

Hillary Clinton was greatly influenced by the theologies of Paul Tillich, Reinhold Niebuhr, SØren Kierkegaard, Dietrich Bonheoffer, and Martin Luther King Jr. This kind of faith seeks to reform the world.

4. The Obama kind of faith, moved on by the compulsion for social justice, the confession of a personal faith in Jesus Christ, "a faith that fills the soul."[5]

For us to properly understand Obama's kind of faith, Mansfield reminds us that first of all, we must note that Obama is "the mulatto child born to an atheist home and to a mother whose baby-boomer wanderings sometimes left the family on food stamps."[6]

In other words, Obama was not born with a silver spoon in his mouth; he was born poor. His own father had left him when he was young. His maternal grandmother raised him. However, by good preparation and hard work, Obama made it through Columbia and Harvard. He became a lawyer and a Christian.

Thus, Obama represents a generation in which faith must bring about a revolution—a change we can believe in. This change we can believe in became Obama's political campaign slogan. This is the kind of faith fit for our age, our nation, and fit for your personal success.

Now, I must say that Obama's kind of faith is both *regenerational* and *transformational*. Regenerational faith can save your soul and take you to heaven. But a transformational faith impacts and affects the entire society. It is the kind of faith that impacts economics, politics, and the environment.

Transformational faith is the kind that turns a microfinanced company into a *macro*financed corporation, a small business outfit into a conglomerate, a small national operative into a multinational corporation (MNC). It is the kind of faith that can make a company like *BusinessDay*, a global competitor with J. P. Morgan Chase, or the *Financial Times* of London.

A transformational faith is the kind of faith that is fueled and propelled by the maxim "Expect great things from God" and "Attempt great things for God." We badly need men and women equipped with this transformational kind of faith, not one of mere orthodoxy.

The transformational faith is revolutionary; it is a faith that changes people and places, things and circumstances. It is this kind of faith that will take you from grass to grace and from nothingness to greatness. It is this kind of faith that makes you become somebody: a success.

I believe that this is the kind of faith needed for this hour, especially in Africa —the Obama kind of faith. This kind of faith destroys apathy and cynicism. This is a living faith in a living God.

CHAPTER FIVE

✦

Incorporation of Hope in Faith

Let me reiterate now our familiar text of Hebrews 11:1: "Faith is the substance of things *hoped* for ..." Here we find the incorporation of hope in faith. Faith and hope are interrelated or interconnected. *It is hope that gives to faith its wings.*

The Bible argues that no one hopes for what is already available and certain (Rom. 8: 24–25), but hope always looks to the future. Faith provides the substance or the assurance, the confirmation, the conviction, the proof, the title deed, or the reality of the things we do not see as yet.

It was the senior Reverend Jesse Jackson who, when he ran for the U. S. presidency in the 1980s, popularized the word *hope* by urging Americans to "keep hope alive." And that hope was realized when, on November 4, 2008, Obama won the presidential.

That, perhaps, was the reason why Rev. Jackson was seen on CNN TV shedding tears of joy as it became obvious that, at long last, a black American would become America's president. It is hope that keeps faith marching on through the dark nights of despair.

Now, what really is hope? In an earlier work, I attempted to answer this question. Therefore, without trying to reinvent the wheel, I shall draw largely from that research.[1]

A SECULAR HOPE

According to the philosopher, Dante, the motto on the gates of hell reads, "Abandon hope, all ye who enter here." The brilliant mind of Francis Bacon caused him to determine that "Hope is a good breakfast, but it is a bad supper." The poet Alexander Pope wrote, "Hope springs eternal in the human breast."[2]

Among many people in the world, hope implies the elements of anticipation and expectation. We often hear people say that they are "hoping against hope." They may say that they have a "vain hope." But one author writes that "among men, to hope for a thing is to be uncertain as to attainment, for hope has to do with the future, and any future, man as man can reckon on, is necessarily uncertain."[3]

A BIBLICAL–SPIRITUAL HOPE

Professor Robert E. Luccock, who was Professor Emeritus of Social Ethics at Union Theological Seminary, defined an Old Testament term, *yachal,* as "to wait with hope, with trust and expectation."[4]

Jill Haak Adels, in his book, *The Wisdom of the Saints: An Anthology* (1987), cited Gregory of Nyssa (330–395 AD), as saying that "hope always draws the soul from the beauty that is seen to what is beyond, always kindles the desire for the hidden through what is perceived."[5]

Professor Luccock included hope in his list of the seven "great resources to live from."[6] The Reverend Billy Graham, writing in *Hope for the Troubled Heart* (1991), concurred with Luccock when he stated, "perhaps the greatest psychological, spiritual, and medical need that all people have is the need for hope." And "Hope is both biologically and psychologically vital to man. Men and women must have hope."[7] He observed, "people in the most affluent societies are feeling this sense of despair and hopelessness."[8] It is with this background knowledge that we can understand the spirituality of hope.

The Bible warns us when it says, "if in this life we who are in Christ have only hope, we are of all men most to be pitied" (1 Cor.15:19). Why? Because secular hope deals with and leads to uncertainty. It offers hopelessness. This is the sad end of any atheistic thinking. In the words of William Shakespeare, "Security is mortal's chiefest enemy" since death, the last enemy of all men, will confront us all eventually.

In contrast to the foregoing, we have the testimony of author Adels who wrote:

> The virtue of hope has the possession of God and eternal happiness as its object. Its grounds are God's goodness, his power, his faithfulness, and most specifically, the resurrection of Christ. Without hope, faith is weakened or disappears.[9]

Author Hy Pickering, in 1905, emphatically stated that:

> In the Scriptures hope simply refers to the future, never to the uncertain. We may be as assured of what God has promised as if we already possessed it. The Bible hope is more than a wish or desire: it is the well-grounded expectation of securing something good.[10]

The Christian does not hope for hope's sake; his hope is rooted in the God who cares and who is wholly trustworthy.[11] Above all, the Christian's hope will be the fulfillment of the church's eschatology. Christians are hopeful of the coming of the Day of the Lord, when there will be a new heaven and a new earth. It will be the consummation of the ages.

Professor Luccock said it best when he wrote, "My own hope beyond hopes is an expectation that *whatever may happen*, God's love will not abandon those who wait with hope, and that such love can transfigure all things."[12]

Some self-styled "positivists" may tell us that this world is getting better and better. I have already lived long enough to know that this is not so. Morally speaking, our world is getting worse and worse, with many heinous crimes like murders, genocides, state-sponsored terrorism, armed robberies, sexual harassments, and rapes reported every day.

These "superficial optimists," as the great preacher Harry Emerson Fosdick called them, are only deceiving themselves if they have not anchored their hope in Jesus Christ. Soon, and very soon, it will all be over. Then, the kingdom of God and of His Christ shall be ushered in.

The gospel news is this: that Christians are "looking for that blessed hope and the glorious appearance of the great God and our Savior Jesus Christ" (Titus 2:13). This hope is about the personal and physical return of Jesus Christ back to this world.

And, until that day dawns, Christians worldwide will continue to unite in that holy prayer that says: "Even so, come quickly, Lord Jesus, come" (Rev. 22:20). This is the Christian's *only* hope and none other. This is the believer's solid rock and expectation.

Hy Pickering stated that there are eight varieties of this biblical or Christian hope, namely:

o   A good hope
o   A living hope
o   A sure hope
o   A purifying hope
o   A blessed hope
o   A non-shaming hope
o   A Christ-honoring hope
o   A Christ-centered hope.[13]

This is the hope of certainty, or, should I say, certitude. The true believer is not beating about the bush. He or she may be called all kinds of names: an escapist from reality, a wishful thinker, an ignoramus, and a blinded, misguided fanatic. But deep down in his or her heart, the Holy Ghost assures that Christ shall one day return to take His people home.

This is what is theologically known as the *rapture* (I Thess. 4:13–18). It is this kind of hope, working with faith in God, which guarantees *good* success. It is this kind of hope and faith that sustains prosperity.

CHAPTER SIX

✦

Obama's "Audacity of Hope"

Since faith and hope are interconnected, it is pertinent here to discuss Obama's "audacity of hope" and to learn one or two things from it. We should keep in mind that Hebrews 11, verse 1 says that faith is the *substance* of things *hoped* for, the evidence of things not seen.

I like the manner in which the Amplified version of the Bible renders this same verse:

> Now faith is the assurance (the confirmation, the title deed) of the things [we] hope for, being the proof of things [we] do not see and the conviction of their reality [faith perceiving as real fact what is not revealed to the senses].

Here, we find that faith and hope are interrelated.

Until July 27, 2004, to be sure, very few people in the United States had ever heard of a Kenyan African American man named Barack Hussein Obama, a state senator from Illinois. But on that July day in Boston, Massachusetts, Obama powerfully delivered the now-famous keynote address titled "The Audacity of Hope." He spoke of "the true genius of America, a faith"—

> a faith in simple dreams, an insistence on small
> miracles; that we can tuck in our children at night
> and know that they are fed and clothed and safe
> from harm; that we can say what we think, write
> what we think, without hearing a sudden knock
> on the door; that we can have an idea and start
> our own business without paying a bribe; that we
> can participate in the political process without
> fear of retribution, and that our votes will be
> counted—at least most of the time.[1]

Read this summary of what makes America unique, again and
again. For it was upon this premise and political understanding
that Obama based his engagement in the change we can believe
in. Most likely, Obama would not have made it in present-day
Nigeria! As I said earlier, Obama's address became the genesis
of his best-selling book, which was published two years later in
2006.

But if you are looking for a masterly definition of the concept
of hope, you will not find it in *The Audacity of Hope*. In fact, in
the index to his book (on page 370), it appears that Obama did
not even use the word in his book! However, he does use the
word *hopeful* when he discusses the legacy that he ought to leave
behind "that will make our children's lives more hopeful than
our own."[2]

Obama uses the phrase *hoped for* in his discussion of faith
in chapter six. He reveals that he believes in the life after death
but he "wasn't sure what happens when we die, anymore than I
was sure of where the soul resides or what existed before the Big
Bang."[3]

This admission is interesting because Obama is a Christian
who believes that his "mother was together in some way with
[his] little girls," and "capable in some fashion of embracing them,
of finding joy in their spirits."[4] Obama is unhappy with some
"inauthentic expressions of faith."[5] These inauthentic expressions

may be seen when a politician suddenly appears at a black church "around election time and claps (off rhythm) to the gospel choir or sprinkles in a few biblical citations to spice up a thoroughly dry policy speech."[6]

The Audacity of Hope is not an analysis of the concept of hope, either theologically or philosophically. Rather, it is about Obama's "thoughts on reclaiming the American dream," as the subtitle declares. These thoughts include American values, the American Constitution, politics, opportunity, faith, race, international affairs, and the American family.[7]

Obama's book calls for a new kind of politics—the change we can believe in. It is dedicated to his mother and his maternal grandmother, the two women who raised him. It should, however, not be forgotten that Obama, in his first book, paid tribute to his father's influence on him during the few years that he was around in the home. *The Audacity of Hope* is actually his political manifesto.

CHAPTER SEVEN

✦

Relevance of Faith to Success

Now that we know and understand what faith is, we can appreciate its relevance to success. We ought to seriously consider this matter because it might just be the reason why we've not yet reached our highest potential and level of success.

Let me repeat what I said earlier: It is nearly impossible to succeed in any significant endeavor without faith. Think about it. Diffidence, the opposite of confidence, will not help you. Neither will fatalism, the idea that "what will be will be." Fatalistic people often fall prey to the curses of superstition and fear. And nihilism is a journey straight into the schoolhouse of cynicism.

Bear in mind that the Bible states that "as a person *thinks* in his or her heart, so is he or she" (Prov. 23:7). Simply put, if you think failure, you will fail; but if you think success and act on your positive thoughts, you will succeed. That is what this text says. So, whatever a person can conceive, dream of, and visualize, he or she can accomplish.

In what ways is faith relevant to success? Consider with me the following **ten** ways:

1. The first area is in obtaining *results*. Both faith and success expect that the proposed line of action will bring about some results. Perhaps this is why, as Victor Hugo is credited with saying, everything bows to success.

Alexander Dumas the Elder is quoted as saying that nothing succeeds like success.

In fact, authentic faith, as we have seen, demands *substance* or the *evidence* of the things that the eyes have not yet seen. Believe me, people who possess faith expect some results from their actions and it is these results that we call success.

2. Faith and success are not only results-oriented, but such results must be *concrete*. The product or substance ought to be measurable, or in some way identifiable. Authentic faith and success will never leave you in a dreamland where you wander about endlessly and aimlessly.

   This is why, in my opinion, some forms of religious teaching and practice are dangerous. Take, for example, the recent case of some so-called Christian ministers who accused innocent children of being witches. A newspaper report in Nigeria stated that a pastor murdered—yes, murdered—one hundred innocent children for allegedly committing the sin of witchcraft!

   Now, we have to ask, "Where is the concrete proof that those children were witches?" Even if they were, should our civilized and modern minds allow us to kill over one hundred of our children? Who gave that pastor the authority to take the lives of those children? Is murder the manner in which Jesus Christ, the one the pastor claimed he served, would have treated them?

3. Faith and success are *positive* phenomena. Authentic faith says: "With God, all things are possible." Success replies: "I am the evidence or the substance of your

faith." Because the end is positive, it is, therefore, not counterproductive.

Whenever you engage in a faith situation, you ought to ask yourself: "Will the outcome be positive and harmless?" If your answer is in the affirmative, then proceed. As a rule, remember this: "God is not in the business of evildoing." God is a very good God. He is an excellent God.

Therefore, the faith and actions that flow forth from Him must be good. The Bible says that God's eyes are so pure that they cannot behold iniquity (Hab. 1:13). The Bible also says that God loves to give *good* things to His children. So, when you exercise faith, know that you are pleasing God (Heb. 11:6) and that your faith is related to something good.

4. Faith and success are *utilitarian*, that is to say, they are useful and beneficial. There is no harm with authentic faith. Although there is such a thing as *bad* success, authentic faith will work with the virtue of wisdom to guide you along the path of *good* success.

    In my book, *Recipe For Success* (2004), I defined success as the accumulation of good deeds, doing one good thing, one at a time.[1] I also believe that success is discovering one's purpose or mission in life and fulfilling that purpose. The ultimate success is to discover the will of God for one's life and to fulfill it.

    With this kind of definition for success, my faith energizes me to work for the glory of God and the betterment of mankind. This is my life's motto. I have a consuming passion to do only those things that are useful or beneficial to humanity. If you share a similar kind of vision, email me and let's be partners in the service of mankind.

5. Faith and success demand *diligence* in our lives. Diligent people are people who work very hard, are careful and thorough. Early in my life, I memorized this important Scripture: "Seest thou a man diligent in his business? He shall stand before kings; he shall not stand before mean men" (Prov. 22: 29).

My understanding of the word *mean* here is mediocre, less than average, ordinary, or common. The diligent man or woman has no business hanging out with the lazy, yawning drones, the mediocre, and the less-than-average. They can and will probably pull him down.

But notice that it is diligence, the by-product of faith, which propels such a person to the great height of success —dinner with royalty or the "Who's Who" of the society. Every successful person that reads this understands what I am talking about.

6. Faith is also relevant to success in the area of one's *outlook* upon life. I would like to call this destiny or worldview.[2] Authentic faith is a faith that looks forward. In other words, within it, there is hope of success. There is nothing like "vain hope," but a hope that offers the assurance that, with God on our side, everything will work out well.

We have the word of Scripture in support of this perspective. It says, "And we know that all things work together for good to them that love God, to them who are the called according to his purpose" (Rom. 8:28).

Do you love God or do you despise and hate Him? If you love Him, then this promise is for you to claim and trust Him for the outcome of whatever situation you are in that you are releasing faith for. Always remember that faith works.

7. The seventh area in which faith is relevant to success is in the matter of *time*. Faith is not an endless cycle of wishes or expectations. Success involves proper time management. As we have seen, faith is the *substance* and to produce a substance involves time. In any matter that produces success, time also is involved.

In the sixth chapter of <u>*Recipe For Success*</u>, I have discussed the issue of time management as a principle for success.[3] Authentic faith will not let you ride a horse endlessly until you arrive at nirvana. No, sir. Time is money!

8. *Decisiveness* is another area in which faith is relevant to success. Although some religious gurus may not agree with me, I believe that authentic faith is intolerant of procrastination, which my pastor says is the thief of time. Most successful people also are intolerant of procrastinators or the people who cannot make quick, good decisions.

Successful and well-run corporations do not pay huge amounts of money to their CEOs so that they may sit at their desks star-gazing over business decisions that should be made quickly. Time-abusers are particularly annoying to successful people.

A story is told of a man who was asked to offer a prayer at a Billy Graham crusade. This man went on and on without stopping. Suddenly, Graham jumped to his feet while the man was still praying and began to preach.

Obviously, this man got his lesson on time management and will never repeat the mistake he had made publicly that day. Authentic faith cares about the use of time and so does success.

9. *Spirituality* is the next area that is relevant to faith and success. Faith is fundamentally a spiritual thing.[4] But may I say to you that often religious people have corrupted this spirituality. Success is also a spiritual thing. It is not entirely a secular or materialistic thing, as many may suppose.

    There is a "theology of success" which I have spoken on at some churches. There is also a theology of money as well as an economic theology. In my book, *What's So Good About Christianity?* I cited the wonderful words credited to John Kenneth Galbraith, the Harvard University economist who said "a man cannot live without an economic theology."[5]

    Definitely, there is a theology of success that has spirituality at its roots. This is derived from all that the sacred books have to say about money, riches, wealth, and wealth acquisition. Those who often ignore this spiritual component often get lost in the sea of mundane concerns. What a tragedy!

10. *Personal fulfillment* is the tenth area in which faith is relevant to success. Faith, from the testimonies of countless men and women, is a fulfilling experience. So also is success. Indeed, faith enhances the opportunities of real success, which can lead to self-actualization.

There may be other areas that show the relevance of faith to human success. But the foregoing ten areas are offered in order to show that faith and success are interrelated, interconnected, and relevant to each other. The compartmentalization of faith and success into sacred and secular need not be so always.

This writer believes that faith, hope, and success are crucial to human and societal development. You'll have to decide whether your kind of faith is working for you or against you. *The audacity of faith is the best friend of success.*

CHAPTER EIGHT

✦

You've Got to Succeed

We have now come to the end of this short but powerful book. May I earnestly say to you that you've got to set your face like a flint to succeed in life. Failure is not an option. In 1999, Tommy Newberry authored a book titled, *Success Is Not an Accident: Change Your Choices, Change Your Life.*[1] You ought to read it.

I urge you to remember the great words of Henry David Thoreau when he said that men are born to succeed, not to fail. Remember also the words by the pastor of the Crystal Cathedral in California, televangelist Dr. Robert Schuller, who said that it is impossible to be a total failure and it is impossible to succeed perfectly. Washington Irving is credited with saying that great minds have purposes, others have wishes.

It may be that you think that you are already a terrible failure and that there is no hope for you to become a success in this life. Listen to me carefully. I was not born with a silver spoon in my mouth. Neither was Barack Obama. My early life was surrounded by crickets, rats, and squirrels at the farms, and by snakes and roaches in our mud-and-wattle, thatched-roof house.

For years, my right arm was my pillow as I slept on a mat without a mattress. My bathroom was often at the Imo River near our home, some fifteen miles from the garden city of Port Harcourt, one of Nigeria's shipping ports. I rarely visited this city.

I walked for about five miles to school each day and five miles back, without shoes in hot tropical weather. Often, I ran back from school to our farm, to meet with my parents who toiled daily from sunup to sundown. Believe me when I say that I used to think that poverty was my birthright. I did not know any better because my parents did not allow us to mingle, even with our next-door neighbors.

So I grew up the shiest and most timid boy that God ever created. But I thank God that my parents allowed me to believe in God quite early in my life. This belief made the difference and it's the secret of my success. As a child, I could not have imagined going to a university in the United States of America! My parents could not have paid the airfare to Lagos, at the time the capital of Nigeria.

But as Oprah Winfrey wrote to me in a letter: "With hard work and a little luck, you can succeed." I discovered that she was right. Even a great part of this book that you are holding in your hands was written in 2008 by torchlight in Lagos, where electricity is rarely available. But this is part of my training in perseverance and persistence. I love what I do—reading and writing books. I cannot imagine a life without books.

Are you still not convinced that you can succeed? Let me tell you of a man called Abraham Lincoln from the state of Illinois, the same state where Barack Obama spent a large portion of his life. You ought to read one of the biographies of Lincoln for inspiration. I would like to share just a little about his life's experiences:

- At age 22, he failed in business.
- At age 23, he ran for the legislature and was defeated.
- At age 24, he attempted business again and failed again.
- At age 25, he was elected to the legislature.
- At age 26, his fiancée died before they could wed.
- At age 27, he had a nervous breakdown.
- At age 29, he was defeated when he ran for House Speaker.

- At age 31, he was defeated when he ran for the Elector.
- At age 34, he was defeated for a congressional office.
- At age 37, he was elected to Congress.
- At age 39, he was defeated again for a congressional office.
- At age 46, he was defeated for the office of senator.
- At age 47, he was defeated for the office of vice president.
- At age 49, he was defeated again for the office of senator.
- At age 51, he was elected to the U.S. presidency.[2]

Lincoln's wife was terrible in her contempt for her husband. She always felt that she was better than him. But she was never the president. And finally, Lincoln was murdered after his victory over the rebels in the American Civil War (1860–1865). This is the man who left us with those immortal words that government needs to be "of the people, by the people, and for the people"—the simplest and easiest definition for democracy.

This is the summary of the life struggles and successes of Abraham Lincoln. Notice that thirteen times Lincoln was defeated or failed over something. He had every reason to give up or quit. But he must have realized that *Quitters never win* and *Winners never quit.*

Lincoln persisted and persevered. How? By the audacity of his faith. He is now considered one of the most respected of all U.S. presidents. You, too, can put your name into the history books by *the audacity of your faith.* It is never too late.

Notes

CHAPTER ONE

1. The Obama historiography is slowly but steadily emerging. See, for example: Barack Obama, *The Audacity of Hope: Thoughts on Reclaiming the American Dream* (New York: Three Rivers Press, 2006), p. 354; and *Dreams From My Father: A Story of Race and Inheritance* (New York: Three Rivers Press, 2004, 1995).

   Other writers on Obama include: Garen Thomas, *Yes We Can: A Biography of Barack Obama* (New York: Feiwel and Friends, 2008); Stephen Mansfield, *The Faith of Barack Obama* (Nashville: Thomas Nelson, 2008); David Mendell, *Obama: A Promise of Change* (New York: Amistad, 2008); Shelby Steele, *A Bound Man: Why We Are Excited About Obama and Why He Can't Win* (New York: Free Press, 2008); Chris Wilson, ed., *Obamamania! The English Language, Barackafield* (New York: Simon & Schuster, 2008); John R. Talbott, *Obamanomics: How Bottom-Up Economic Prosperity Will Replace Trickle-Down Economics* (New York: Seven Stories Press, 2008); John K. Wilson, *Barack Obama: The Improbable Quest* (Boulder, CO & London: Paradigm Publishers, 2008); David Freddoso, *The Case Against Barack Obama: The Unlikely Rise and Unexamined Agenda of the Media's Favorite Candidate* (Washington DC: Regnery Publishers, 2008); Jerome R. Corsi, *The Obama Nation: Leftist Politics and the Cult of Personality* (New York: Threshold Editions, 2008); Ben Anagwonye, ed., *Greatest Speeches of Historic Black Leaders: Barack Obama, Martin Luther King Jr., Nelson Mandela, Jesse Jackson* (Benin, Nigeria: Mindex Publishing, 2008); David Mendell, *Obama: From Promise to Power* (New York: Amistad, 2007); Lisa Rogak, ed., *Barack Obama in His Own Words* (New York: Carroll and Graf Publishers, 2007); and Steve Dougherty, *Hopes and Dreams: The Story of Barack Obama* (New York: Black Dog and Leventhal Publishers, 2007). More of these materials are in the bibliography at the end of this book.

Obama has appeared in *too* many magazines and newspapers for us to mention all of them. The following are just a few to note: *Rolling Stone*; *Men's Vogue*; *Harper's*; *Us Weekly*; *Newsweek*; *Time*; *Ebony*; *The Black EOE Journal*; *Black Enterprise*; and *Jet*. Obama is often on the front-page cover of these magazines.

Newspaper coverage of Obama prior to his election victory included the New York *Daily News* and the *Washington Post*. It would not be an exaggeration to say that almost every newspaper in America has featured a story on Obama. Thus, Obama has become a brand name and he may be the most globally covered U.S. president in history, even before he took the office.

2. Cosmas Maduka, "Audacity of Dreams," *The Daily Sun* (December 14, 2008), 21.
3. Ibid. 25.
4. Felix Meduoye, "The Audacity of Faith," *Sunday Sun* (December 14, 2008), 50.
5. Minabere Ibelema, "Audacity of Corruption: U.S. vs. Nigeria," *Sunday Punch* opinion (December 14, 2008), 20.

6. Daniel Alabrah, Willy Eya, Mike Jimoh, and Paul Obadan, "Audacity of Hope! Can Nigeria Achieve It Here?" *Sunday Sun* (November 9, 2008), 1, 9–10, and 15.
7. Ibid. 9.
8. Karen C. Aboiralor, "Nigeria: 'The Audacity of Hope.'" (Abuja) *Leadership* (December 31, 2008), 1–3.
9. Ibid.
10. Kemi Ajumobi, "Etuk's Take on the 'audacity of faith,'" *BusinessDay* (December 12–14, 2008), 16.

CHAPTER TWO

1. *The Longman Dictionary of Contemporary English*, 3rd ed., (Essex, UK: Pearson Education Ltd., 2000), 71.
2. Ibid. (underlining added)
3. Ibid., 1485.
4. Ibid., 443.
5. Ibid., 635.
6. W. F. Kumuyi, *Have Compassion on Them* (Lagos: Life Press Ltd., 1991), 75.

CHAPTER THREE

1. Many writers whose works are cited in the bibliography have answered this question. See also: J. Gresham Machen, *What Is Faith?* (New York: The Macmillan Co., 1925); Harry E. Fosdick, *The Meaning of Faith* (New York: Association Press, 1921, 1918); Ney Bailey, *Faith Is Not a Feeling: Choosing to Take God at His Word* (Colorado Springs, CO: Waterbrook Press, 2002); and Allan A. Hunter, *The Audacity of Faith* (New York: Harper and Brothers, 1949).
2. Smith Wigglesworth, *The Power of Faith* (Springdale, PA: Whitaker House, 2000); Paul Tillich, *Dynamics of Faith* (New York: Harper Perennial, 1986); and Reinhard

Bonnke, *Faith: The Link with God's Power* (Nashville: Nelsonword Publishing Group, 1998).

3. James W. Fowler, *Stages of Faith: The Psychology of Human Development* (New York: HarperOne, 1995); B. B. Warfield, *Faith and Life* (Edinburgh: Banner of Truth, 1974); Billy Graham, *The Journey: How to Live by Faith in an Uncertain World* (Nashville: Thomas Nelson, 2006); and Terry Pluto, *Faith and You* (Cleveland, OH: Gray and Co., Publishers, 2005).

4. Krista Tippett, *Speaking Faith* (New York: Viking, 2007), Dale A. Matthews, *The Faith Factor: Proof of the Healing Power of Prayer* (New York: Viking, 1998); and Dorothy C. Bass, ed., *Practicing Our Faith: A Way of Life for a Searching People* (San Francisco: Jossey Bass Inc., 1997).

5. Jim Cymbala and Dean Merrill, *Fresh Faith: What Happens When Real Faith Ignites God's People* (Grand Rapids, MI: Zondervan, 1999).

Chapter Four

1. This is the title of one of Zig Ziglar's books, *See You At the Top* (Gretna, LA: Pelican Publishing Co., 2000).
2. Stephen Mansfield, *The Faith of Barack Obama*, 104.
3. Ibid., 108.
4. Ibid., 110.
5. Ibid., 109.
6. Ibid., 102.

Chapter Five

1. Emma S. Etuk, *What's So Good About Christianity? Five Amazing Ways the Gospel Has Influenced and Blessed Our Lives* (Washington DC: Emida International Publishers, 2000), 38–42.
2. Peter McWilliams, *The Life 101 Quote Book* (Los Angeles: Prelude Press, 1996), 121–123.

3. Etuk, *What's So Good*, 39.
4. Ibid.
5. Ibid.
6. Ibid.
7. Ibid., 38
8. Ibid.
9. Ibid., 39.
10. Ibid., 40.
11. Ibid.
12. Ibid.
13. Ibid., 42.

CHAPTER SIX

1. Ben Anagwonye, *Greatest Speeches*, 3.
2. Obama, *The Audacity of Hope*, 361.
3. Ibid., 226.
4. Ibid.
5. Ibid., 215–216.
6. Ibid., 216
7. See the Table of Contents in Obama, *The Audacity of Hope*.

CHAPTER SEVEN

1. Emma S. Etuk, *Recipe for Success: The 21 Indispensable Things That Can Help You Succeed in Life* (Washington DC: Emida International Publishers, 2004), front jacket flyleaf.
2. Ibid., 201–208.
3. Ibid., 65–72.
4. Ibid., 89–103.
5. John K. Galbraith, cited in Etuk, *What's So Good About Christianity?*, 113.

Chapter Eight

1. See Tommy Newberry, *Success Is Not an Accident: Change Your Choices, Change Your Life* (Decatur, GA: Looking Glass Books, 1999).
2. Etuk, *Recipe For Success*, 78–79.

Selected Bibliography

Books

Asim, Jabari. *What Obama Means for Our Culture, Our Politics, Our Future.* New York: William Morrow, 2009.

Berkhof, Hendrikus. *Christian Faith: An Introduction to the Study of the Faith.* Grand Rapids, MI: William B. Eerdmans, 1979.

Capps, Charles. *Faith and Confession: How to Activate the Power of God in Your Life.* Tulsa, OK: Harrison House, 1994.

Carlton, Bob, and Ariele Gentiles. *Barack Obama: An American Story.* Grand Rapids, MI: Zondervan, 2008.

Carwardine, Richard. *Lincoln: A Life of Purpose and Power.* New York: Alfred A. Knopf, 2006.

Delingpole, James. *Welcome to Obamaland: I Have Seen Your Future and It Doesn't Work.* Washington DC: Regnery Publishing, 2009.

Dulles, Avery. *The Assurance of Things Hoped For: A Theology of Christian Faith.* New York: Oxford University Press, 1997.

Edwards, Roberta. *Barack Obama: An American Story.* New York: Grosset and Dunlap, 2008.

Ellul, Jacques. *Hope in Time of Abandonment*. New York: The Seabury Press, 1973.

Gilmore, G. Don. *No Matter How Dark the Valley: The Power of Faith in Times of Need*. New York: Harper and Row, 1982.

Gormley, Beatrice. *Barack Obama: Our 44th President*. New York: Aladdin, 2008.

Green, Mark, and Michele Jolin, eds. *Change for America: A Progressive Blueprint for the 44th President*. New York: Perseus, 2009.

Heschel, Abraham Joshua. *Moral Grandeur and Spiritual Audacity: Essays*. New York: Farrar, Straus, and Giroux, 1997.

Hill, Brennan, William Madges, and Paul F. Knitter. *Faith, Religion and Theology: A Contemporary Introduction*. Mystic, CT: Twenty-Third Publications, 1997, 1990.

Hinckley, Gordon B. *Faith: The Essence of True Religion*. Salt Lake City: Deseret Book, 1989.

Ifill, Gwen. *The Break-Through: Politics and Race in the Age of Obama*. New York: Doubleday, 2009.

Ignatius, Idi, ed. *President Obama: The Path to the White House*. New York: Time, 2008.

Leanne, Shel. *Say It Like Obama: The Power of Speaking with Purpose and Vision*. New York: McGraw-Hill, 2009.

Lightfoot, Elizabeth. *Michelle Obama: First Lady of Hope*. Guilford, CT: The Lyons Press, 2009.

Macquarrie, John. *Christian Hope*. New York: The Seabury Press, 1978.

McLaren, Brian. D. *Finding Faith: A Self-Discovery Guide for Your Spiritual Quest*. Grand Rapids, MI: Zondervan, 1999.

Meland, Bernard Eugene. *Faith and Culture*. Carbondale: Southern Illinois University Press, 1953.

Nelson, Kadir. *Change Has Come: An Artist Celebrates Our American Spirit*. New York: Simon & Schuster, 2009.

Obama, Barack. *Change We Can Believe In: Barack Obama's Plan to Renew America's Promise*. New York: Three Rivers Press, 2008.

Ortberg, John. *Faith and Doubt*. Grand Rapids, MI: Zondervan, 2008.

Oursler, Fulton. *The Greatest Faith Ever Known*. New York: Doubleday, 1953.

Phipps, Wintley. *The Power of a Dream: The Inspiring Story of a Young Man's Audacious Faith*. Grand Rapids, MI: Zondervan, 1994.

Plantinga, Alvin. *Faith and Rationality: Reason and Belief in God*. Notre Dame, IN: University of Notre Dame Press, 1983.

Price, Charles S. *The Real Faith for Healing*. Gainesville, FL: Bridge-Logos Publishers, 1997.

———. *The Meaning of Faith: A Classic Writing on the Mystery of Faith*. Nashville: Mercyplace Ministries, 2002.

Price, Frederick K. C. *Faith's Greatest Enemies*. Tulsa, OK: Harrison House, 1994.

———. *How to Obtain Strong Faith: Six Principles*. Tulsa, OK: Harrison House, 2002.

———. *How Faith Works*. Los Angeles, CA: Frederick K. C. Price Ministries, 2002.

Prince, Derek. *Faith to Live By*. Springdale, PA: Whitaker House, 1999.

Reeve, Pamela. *Faith Is*. New York: Doubleday, 2004.

Sanger, David E. *The Inheritance: The World Obama Confronts and the Challenges to American Power*. New York: Harmony Books, 2009.

Sproul, R. C. *Faith Alone: The Evangelical Doctrine of Justification*. Grand Rapids, MI: Baker, 1995.

Thomas, Evan. *"A Long Time Coming." The Inspiring, Combative 2008 Campaign and the Historic Election of Barack Obama*. New York: Public Affairs, 2009.

Tinder, Glenn E. *The Fabric of Hope: An Essay*. Grand Rapids, MI: William B. Eerdmans, 1999.

Tozer, A. W. *Faith Beyond Reason*. Camp Hill, PA: Christian Publications, 1989.

Tufankjian, Scout. *Yes We Can: Barack Obama's History-Making Presidential Campaign.* New York: Melcher Media Inc., 2008.

Wigglesworth, Smith. *Ever Increasing Faith*. Springfield, MO: Gospel Publishing House, 1971.

Winter, Jonah. *Barack*. New York: HarperCollins, 2008.

Wolpe, David J. *Why Faith Matters*. New York: HarperOne, 2008.

ARTICLES

Ajumobi, Kemi. "Etuk's Take on the 'Audacity of Faith.'" *BusinessDay*, December 12–14, 2008.

Chapman, Steve. "The Audacity of America." *RealClear Politics*, November 6, 2008.

Darner, Michael. "The Audacity of Faith." *Center for Competitive Politics*, February 27, 2008.

Driscoll, Ed. "The Audacity of Blind Faith." *EdDriscoll.com*, June 5, 2008.

Emereuwa, Kinsley. "Ochendo: The Audacity of Faith." *Daily Sun*, August 7, 2008.

Falsani, Cathleen. "The Audacity of Faith." *Google Groups*, October 26, 2008.

Fonkem, Sam Nuvala. "Africa: Snapshot—The Audacity of Obama." *ThePostnewsline.com*, November 7, 2008.

Gerson, Michael. "The Audacity of Cynicism." *WashingtonPost Writers Group*, July 2, 2008.

Gilbert, Steve. "Obama's Audacity—Bringing Us Together." *Bookmark*, March 13, 2008.

Griffin, Leslie J. "Faith: A Vehicle That Gives Strength and Hope to the Unknown." *Michigan Chronicle*, March 26, 2008.

Hall, Mike. "The Audacity of Faith." *Culture_11*, September 12, 2008.

Hilario, Frank A. "The Audacity of Love." *American Chronicle*, November 24, 2008.

Ittycheria, Dev. "The Audacity of Faith." *SiliconIndia*, 2008.

Marcus, Ruth. "The Audacity of Nope." *Washingtonpost.com*, January 3, 2007.

McElvaine, Robert S. "The Audacity of Dope." *Huffingtonpost. com*. Inc., July 27, 2008.

McWhorter, John H. "The Audacity of Pragmatism." *www. theRoot.com,* July 9, 2008.

Murphy, Kirk James. "The Audacity of Hate: Obama Elevates 'Coincidental' Eliminationist, Hallelujah." *Firedoglake*, August 16, 2008.

North, Gary. "The Audacity of Hype." *www.garynorth.com*, January 20, 2009.

Nyatsine, Lovemore. "The Audacity of Faith and Hope." *The Zimbabwe Guardian*, November 11, 2008.

Oyakhilome, Chris. "The Audacity of Faith." Audiotape, *Christ Embassy*, 2009.

Patrick, Rod. "The Audacity of Barack Obama's Arrogance: Obama's Latest Gaffe—A Sign of Megalomania." _www.redstate.com_, September 25, 2008.

Sabar, Ariel. "Barack Obama: Putting Faith Out Front." _The Christian Science Monitor_, July 16, 2007.

Sabater, Liza. "The Audacity of Biracial Hope." _Culture Kitchen_, January 7, 2008.

Sanusi, Ruka. "The Audacity of Faith … and Love." _The Art of Living_, February 18, 2008.

Shafran, Avi. "The Audacity of Hopelessness." _Cross-Currents_, December 12, 2008.

Shirley, Jerry. "Audacity of Faith: Obama Mocks the Holy Bible," AVS Audiotape, _www.AudacityofHypocrisy.com_, August 6, 2008.

———. "Change We Can Believe in: The Audacity of Faith." _Grace Notes Ministries_, n.d.

Sina, Ali. "The Audacity of Frauds." _www.Faithfreedom.org_, October 27, 2008.

Sullivan, Andrew. "The Audacity of Faith." _The Atlantic_, April 13, 2008.

"The Audacity of Faith." _Resounding Truth_, December 31, 2008.

"The Audacity of Hypocrisy." Opinion, _Washington Blade_, October 26, 2007.

Yoest, Jack and Charmaine. "Reasoned Audacity! Business and Politics in Real Life." *www.charmaineyoest.com*, December 22, 2006.

NEWSPAPERS

Saturday *Independent*, November 15, 2008.

The Nation, October 26, 2008.

The Nation, November 21, 2008.

Punch, November 24, 2008.

Sunday *Punch*, November 9, 2008,

Sunday *Punch*, November 16, 2008.

Sunday *Punch*, November 30, 2008.

The *Punch*, November 10, 2008.

Sunday *Sun*, November 2, 2008.

About the Author

Best-selling and award-winning author, international motivational speaker, and professional historian, Emma Samuel Etuk is the president of Emida International Publishers. A graduate of Howard University in Washington DC, he obtained his PhD in United States History, with minors in African History and International Relations.

Etuk is the recipient of many awards, including the 2005 Irwin Award for the Best International Campaign; the LABBE Award (2005) in recognition of his distinguished achievement for *Recipe For Success*, a book which now sells in six countries; and the 2005 Akwa Ibom State Association of Nigeria (USA), Inc. Leadership Award, in recognition of his exemplary leadership in the community. In 1999, Etuk and his family were honored at the U.S. Congress as "Parents of the Year" for the state of Maryland.

He resides with his family in Forestville, Maryland. *The Audacity of Faith* is his eleventh book. He may be reached by email at emida1@yahoo.com or www.etuk.successuniversity.com, or by telephone at 540-429-2392.